Months of the Year

October

by Robyn Brode

Reading consultant: Susan Nations, M.Ed.,
author/literacy coach/consultant

WEEKLY WR READER®
EARLY LEARNING LIBRARY

Please visit our web site at: www.earlyliteracy.cc
For a free color catalog describing Weekly Reader® Early Learning Library's list
of high-quality books, call 1-877-445-5824 (USA) or 1-800-387-3178 (Canada).
Weekly Reader® Early Learning Library's fax: (414) 336-0164.

Library of Congress Cataloging-in-Publication Data

Brode, Robyn.
    October / by Robyn Brode.
      p. cm. — (Months of the year)
    Summary: An introduction to some of the characteristics, events, and activities
of the month of October.
    ISBN 0-8368-3585-9 (lib. bdg.)
    ISBN 0-8368-3621-9 (softcover)
    1. October—Juvenile literature. 2. Holidays—United States—Juvenile literature.
[1. October.] I. Title.
GT4803.B7695   2003
394.264—dc21

2002034306

First published in 2003 by
Weekly Reader® Early Learning Library
330 West Olive Street, Suite 100
Milwaukee, WI 53212 USA

Copyright © 2003 by Weekly Reader® Early Learning Library

Editor: Robyn Brode
Art direction, design, and page production: Leonardo Montenegro with Orange Avenue
Models: Olivia Byers-Strans, Isabella Leary, Madeline Leary
Weekly Reader® Early Learning Library art direction: Tammy Gruenewald
Weekly Reader® Early Learning Library editor: Mark J. Sachner

Photo credits: Cover, title, pp. 7, 11, 13, 15, 17 © Getty Images; p. 9 © Veer; p. 19
Leonardo Montenegro; p. 21 © Comstock Images

Printed in the United States of America

1 2 3 4 5 6 7 8 9 07 06 05 04 03

Note to Educators and Parents

Reading is such an exciting adventure for young children! They are beginning to integrate their oral language skills with written language. To help this process along, books must be meaningful, colorful, engaging, and interesting; they should invite young readers to make inquiries about the world around them.

Months of the Year is a new series of books designed to help children learn more about each of the twelve months. In each book, young readers will learn about festivals, celebrations, weather, and other interesting facts about each month.

Each book is specially designed to support the young reader in the reading process. The familiar topics are appealing to young children and invite them to re-read — again and again. The full-color photographs and enhanced text further support the student during the reading process.

These books are designed to be read within an instructional guided reading group. This small group setting allows beginning readers to work with a fluent adult model as they make meaning from the text. After children develop fluency with the text and content, the book can be read independently. Children and adults alike will find these books supportive, engaging, and fun!

— *Susan Nations, M.Ed., author, literacy coach,*
and consultant in literacy development

October is the tenth month of the year. October has 31 days.

October

1	2	3	4	5	6	7
8	9	10	11	12	13	14
15	16	17	18	19	20	21
22	23	24	25	26	27	28
29	30	31				

October is a fall month. During this month in some places, leaves fall from trees. It is fun to run and jump in piles of colorful autumn leaves.

It is also fun to take walks in the woods. The leaves smell good and make a crunching sound when you walk on them.

Sometimes there are too many leaves on the ground. When lots of leaves have fallen on the ground, it's time to rake them up.

In some places, the weather has turned cool. It is usually a great time to ride bikes.

What do you like to do best in October?

October 31 is Halloween.
Some kids go to a
pumpkin patch to pick
out pumpkins. It is fun
to see the different sizes
and shapes.

Some kids like to cut out funny faces on pumpkins. There are many funny faces and shapes you can make on a pumpkin.

On Halloween, some kids dress up in costumes and go to parties or go "trick or treating."

What is your favorite Halloween costume?

When October ends,
it is time for November
to begin.

Glossary

autumn leaves — leaves that turn orange, red, and yellow and then fall off trees

pumpkin — a roundish orange vegetable that is ready to pick in the fall

trick or treating — a time on Halloween when kids dress up in costumes and visit their neighbors for gifts of candy and other treats

Months of the Year

1	January	7	July
2	February	8	August
3	March	9	September
4	April	**10**	**October**
5	May	11	November
6	June	12	December

Seasons of the Year

Winter	Summer
Spring	Fall

About the Author

Robyn Brode wrote the *Going Places* children's book series and was the editor for *Get Out!*, which won the 2002 Disney Award for Hands-On Activities. She has been an editor, writer, and teacher in the book publishing field for many years. She earned a Bachelors in English Literature from the University of California at Berkeley.